SONATA IN D
Op. 2, No. 2
for Flute and Piano (with Basso Continuo)

By Michel Blavet
Edited by Louis Moyse

ED 3543

ISBN 978-0-634-00209-0

G. SCHIRMER, Inc.

DISTRIBUTED BY
HAL•LEONARD® CORPORATION
7777 W. BLUEMOUND RD. P.O. BOX 13819 MILWAUKEE, WI 53213

SONATA IN D, Op. 2, No. 2

La Vibray
For Flute and Piano

Michel Blavet
(1700-1768)
Edited by Louis Moyse

* *All trills start from the top note and on the beat.*

48733c

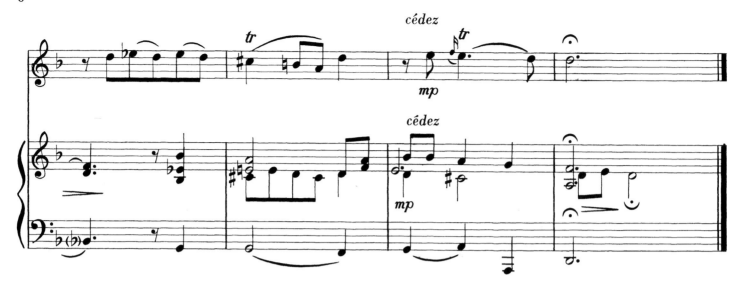

Allemande

Gavotte
Les Caquets

SONATA IN D, Op. 2, No. 2
La Vibray
For Flute and Piano

Flute

Michel Blavet
(1700-1768)
Edited by Louis Moyse

Andante

dolce piano

poco cresc.

(on the beat)

mp

p

10

poco cresc.

mp

mf

20

p

mp

poco cresc.

mp

mf

All trills start from the top note and on the beat.

Flute

Allemande

Flute

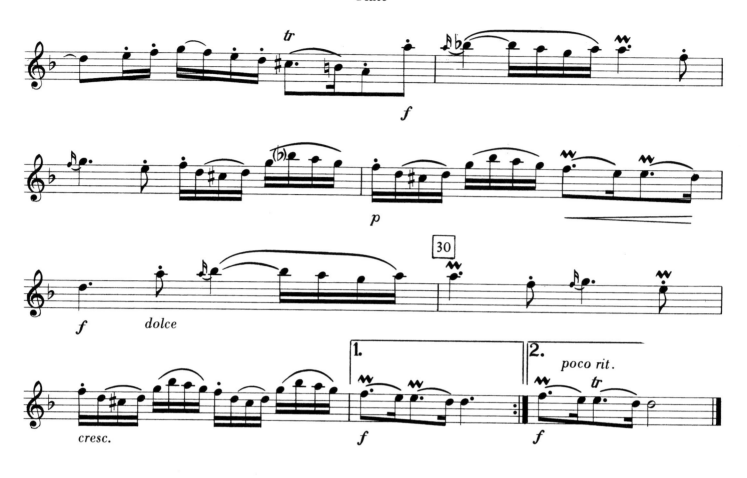

Gavotte
Les Caquets

Sarabande

Finale

poco a poco cresc.

SONATA IN D
Op. 2, No. 2

By Michel Blavet
Edited by Louis Moyse

ED 3543

ISBN 978-0-634-00209-0

G. SCHIRMER, Inc.

DISTRIBUTED BY

HAL•LEONARD®
CORPORATION

7777 W. BLUEMOUND RD. P.O. BOX 13819 MILWAUKEE, WI 53213

SONATA IN D, Op. 2, No. 2
La Vibray
For Flute and Piano

Michel Blavet
(1700-1768)
Edited by Louis Moyse

Basso Continuo

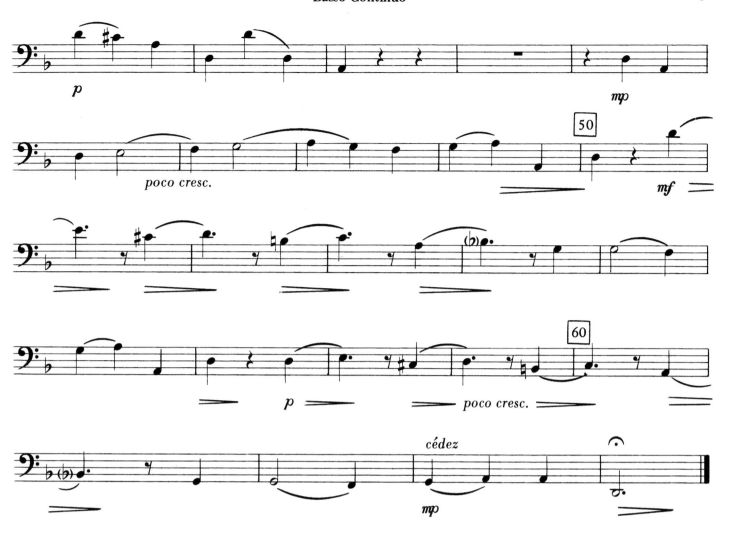

Allemande

Basso Continuo

Gavotte
Les Caquets

Basso Continuo

Sarabande

Basso Continuo

Finale

Sarabande

Finale